# SKY BOOTHS IN THE BREATH SOMEWHERE,

### The ASHBERY ERASURE Poems

## david dodd lee

# SKY BOOTHS IN THE BREATH SOMEWHERE,

The ASHBERY ERASURE Poems

david dodd lee

BlazeVOX [books]

Buffalo, New York

Sky Booths In the Breath Somewhere, by David Dodd Lee

Printed in the United States of America

Book design by Geoffrey Gatza

First Edition
ISBN: 9781935402879
Library of Congress Control Number 2009941036


BlazeVOX [books]
303 Bedford Ave
Buffalo, NY 14216

Editor@blazevox.org

*publisher of weird little books*

# BlazeVOX [ books ]

blazevox.org

2   4   6   8   0   9   7   5   3   1

B           X

# Acknowledgment

The poem "Sin Bird" comes from Ashbery's "Sicilian Bird," published in *SS*.

The poem "Tricycle" comes from Ashbery's "Just for Starters" published in *SS*. I erased the original poem but also re-arranged the lines, etc.

The rest of the poems in this book use Ashbery's own titles (see note beginning on page 13).

Several Ashbery Erasure poems have appeared in *Passages North, Shampoo, The Laurel Review, No Tell Motel,* and *Caffeine Destiny.*

"Tricycle" appeared on *Verse Daily,* April 23, 2007.

Poems in this manuscript used source material from the following John Ashbery books: *(SS) And the Stars were Shining, (HL) Hotel Launtreamont, (FC) Flow Chart,* as well as *(ST) Some Trees, (AWC) A Worldly Country, (AWK) As We Know,* (HD)*Houseboat Days, (W) Wakefulness, (NFA) Notes from the Air.*

# TABLE OF CONTENTS

# SKY BOOTHS IN THE BREATH SOMEWHERE,

## The ASHBERY ERASURE Poems

**Notes On The Text:**

About the Ashbery Erasure poems: It is important to understand that what started as homage-slash-critique evolved—more and more, as I "composed" new poems from the source material—into my own act of creation. There was little to no premeditation in any of this. I was re-reading Ashbery—perhaps with a bit more concentration; sometimes with excitement, sometimes in frustration—and I flushed with the realization that I could extract "poems" from these amazingly circuitous texts, *poems* from *poems*, of course, but poems I truly believed would hold up as strong and unique structures (or lyrics) apart from the source texts. And yet I felt strongly, at times, a sense I was merging with the "ongoingness" of Ashbery's language, and that I was somehow simply containing his horizonless energy in a much smaller space, even as I imagined myself to also be dismantling everything, making something absolutely new out of what stood on the pages before me.

It was a maddeningly wonderful experience.

The rules were simple enough. I could use in these new "poems" any words (or parts of words) from any single Ashbery poem. But I couldn't just pick words randomly from anywhere in the linear thread of words that comprised any given Ashbery poem. I had to construct my text by moving through the source poem, selecting words as Ashbery ordered them (consecutively), while omitting the rest. In other words, were I to white-out my omissions on the page of an Ashbery text one would have little trouble, reading from left to right, deciphering the words and phrases that make up the "narratives" that are my erasure poems.

So, this *was* a process of omission—*erasure*—although complicated by self-interest. The desire to construct new meanings via syntax and content often directed me (more and more so the further I got into the work). I'd create words I felt I wanted/needed by simply reading through a text until I found the letters that made up the word, even if this took me through ten lines worth of poem (which I could then no longer use). And I did arrange what I selected into lines, an act that helped confuse ownership of the resulting poem once it appeared on the printed page (this struggle over ownership became one of the overriding tensions of the project) . . .

In fact, I've discovered--in a couple of instances--that I somehow inadvertently "invented" a letter or two during the process of completing new poems. I left these accidents in place since I never intentionally *added* anything. Erasure typos. In the end these happened infrequently enough to seem worthy of inclusion.

The Ashbery poems I chose to erase I chose quite randomly, sometimes directed by whatever book happened to be at hand (I have different titles at different locations). There was no process in place for this. It was spontaneous, and occasionally I would begin "erasing" (circling and scratching out words right in the book itself), and then discover something didn't feel quite right about what was happening and so I'd pick another poem.

The titles of the poems are usually Ashbery's own. To compare my texts to Ashbery's simply locate the poem by title in Ashbery's books. The exceptions are the poems in which only the first word in the title is capitalized. These texts are culled from single pages in Ashbery's long poem, *Flow Chart*. The titles in these instances were selected from language in the first line, usually, of the source page.

Information about which books the poems came from can be found on the acknowledgments page.

# SKY BOOTHS IN THE BREATH SOMEWHERE,

## The ASHBERY ERASURE Poems

1

# THE ARCHIPELAGO

sisters land
an arson for feeling

so daffodils as nasturtiums come along as a rule

She said, Really, the mind is a waste

but like a sitting arthritic

word like a branch to all the other words

sun following loud behind our basket

undo me!

the islands are shrieking

snug in my unzipped fly

# IN THE MEANTIME, DARLING

Time is a cross

There is a feeling you put on

Listen
Eavesdropping is the only way
You hand over
The sea

Hurricane
A lie and his sister
Sure times

Purity
The others bent for later
No food in his mouth

He comes

Dactyl in the ethnic ballpark

It's better, this ache

# SIN BIRD

The perfume climbs red words
most amply.

Phony people try to hear it
to get away.

Horses through hell,
it's normal.
That summer we rent.

Bugs came and people have cars
to carry them.

And man sets his pet up, artificial,
a photograph,
a car in mist.

Pardon the land or lock us out.

## SOMETIMES IN PLACES

Patient, no poet lies down under the dream.

The sky is cleverer than he.

So what?

The robin builds a nest.

Day weaves a bower.

Self to world: I am standing here listening.

Desire, O accidental man,
the purple plenty dominate our dreams.

Nod and be gay.

You too enter the skirmish of ghosts.

Dragons so blessed with deafness
clamor for lunch.

No, I thought
No, that was mine.

# THE BEER DRINKERS

Think of it as something
merely in the way, go over,
eat it.

Look at this season

Trees draped in umbrellas raw
like beads from a string
subliminal magic.

Just keep out of the way.
Be young.
Final.

Weather as lame, *a crowd*,
and us of course, folks home for the newspaper.

Tell a nurse to color these Americans,
coin extracted from the truth.

Add distance.

Camp embarrassed in a bathrobe.

He was in the rut and he came,
one fat annihilated darling.

# WORKS ON PAPER I

Japan is famous with chairs,
Tall brew around a contradiction.

Now his bus takes him where the perplexed doomed
Get hangovers.  Afternoon souvenir, an arrangement,
Old sea where passengers hang flummoxed.

Ill with looking, an empire is dying.

Between the benign outskirts,
Everyone reasonably free to fall,

The naked are coaxed out with tea,
The shivering trees own the bookstore.

Blow September

Go sing

Before the red dogs are ash.

# STRANGE THINGS HAPPEN AT NIGHT

Think about it
Prepare to go out of your dreams

Art cannot see you

Your boyfriend
Numb
Should've turned by now

Rain impedes recess
We must act remote
Every day

Bicycle
Ribs
People
The hot thought not lost

Go turn up your living

I mean uppers
The odes
Or gas

Man can be made to last

# All at once

eventually rot seeds the ground

rot is a question—

and shot people don't look back at you

I'll have the food—
eyelids for wood

you saw it shut in them

inside every house there's a spotted sun
warm as thunder

all the doors in a flood
it never occurs to the light of the sun
the people are able to sound simple
out the upstairs window

so the loud hen withdrew

no person was actually coming unclear

# Lucky hits

One doesn't excuse or batter
the pupils

I came straight after love and left
shame routed the street
I was a good peasant

so let me bang toward a cock
and its one eye rolling

I don't know what makes
the maker sacred

paste that squeezes our seed

we were not meant to be some problem gone dead

# Buy something

And so never has
already happened.

You can turn off that pet now.

Girls I know were
Boy handed.

one  side  they  sin

my idea of myself does exist
like this thin man

I told the kids the air was nice

cheese for everybody

the knife sat on the lock, a figure
to include

in our bones the big child hits

# In favor of life

nobody knew where to buy a minute
after God was forgotten

long shadows wider each time

names in the fabric like pain

so when will God be able to
disconnect us from all that is real?

you think of desire as a lit stone in hell

my life, what's the point?

it isn't nature

wind is a noise, a thing I'll punish tonight

# What it's worth

you think it's the calm
of day to day, a naïve star,

the past
the waters

not something one lives for

I ask you
who repairs the model
of our loud
white sister

we sleep to rescue no one

Yet time flew over us

sex was coming through with
the usual blossoms

I mean the father can't even wake up

# ERRORS

weather in boxes
lit red with snow

Carnivores, and light

winter is beyond the bed

tall and violent

i thought of your plight
cave doping
a tit of unrisen love

Flat head that fumes
desire for falling

pay her

the rope's silence is true?

# But like the

Torso of a proud
Saving grace

When the men go down no one hears

Flesh is a feeling
Like wind tearing at memory

It's just space

Keep an eye on the appalling
Development which enfolds

Your toes first

Then wake up and seem ordinary

# Later when

it doesn't matter,
my red world

one had the sense to ignore
the enveloping

shroud

everything should erupt

lightning the flavor of blood

war engraved on a teakettle

heaven was to be done
without diluting the whole

rags of old rationale,
a confused box

one longs for hell

that, at any rate, was my winter

2

# THE IMPROVEMENT

I hate this room,
the whole whatever

life beyond
part mind in the moment--

kindly, crazy

enough to smile somehow as we converse

transparent mess
of a dream

even when there's a beating
i want openness

of an unasked question

calculations of heaven

i own the starting gate

# ONE EVENING, A TRAIN

God likes us for ourselves

man
the little strange guest

You're free to love

We've had so little will

black drops of acquittal

a crime witnessed
between Chinese water tortures

yet somewhere, fun will happen because of us . . .

like one long serious breath

and there are men to boil

the scent

I'm afraid

is a temple

# But you think

you keep up with them
conscience and crowd

a bell-jar
wiped clean with suffering

a woman comes quietly
to the glass
transformed into static

you are a voyeur, too
a voyeur trying to kill

the mind, drifting away,
faintly out of tune

no scars
we had the reward of shining

eyes full of cataclysm
a landscape that matters

maybe she will come along
mean
an irritation

her weather is little more
than a groan

# A horn screeched

Particles cannot move
full in sight, gone now

and I am a dog
I can think

I remember once
receiving her swan

convulsive instant dark though a problem

the other wise interruption
so silly
light for five minutes a decade

the facts attach centuries

turn to me
name all I ask

I focus
go down into the vicious city

vibrations and pain

no shopping malls
no houseplants

# I FOUND THEIR ADVICE

language itself

A hanging we cling to

now it is half-past five
the learning has begun

Who weren't learning
stopped knowing
the silence

time as a seal,
contained,
not banked:

you don't jostle
the voice,

and the feelings leave

# WILD BOYS OF THE ROAD

He fell apart
rusting and happy

she was blinkered on the carpet

the result was this heavenly uproar

the trillium has
no excuse
for being here

though perhaps the deep fact
of everything is crazy

boys sleeping beside cattle

a kite-string

and mostly our friends fear us

a church you can destroy
without touching the glossary

I tell you the shouting
is too extreme

the hand is too easy

# A WALTZ DREAM

She was a strange fault
thought for every minor upheaval

It may have been the praying,
white lake like a photograph

of plasma

a man shits cookie cutters

a steamroller lops off nine busboys

in my own dream
I square the imaginary hinge we were meant to oil

mother is mindful of rain
in the mixed drinks

girls like lemonade

# THE LOUNGE

That is if my lord,
lit with secrets,
rested hearty in his lounge

Some prairie in the mural

makes me wrong

the late school brothels

have no peg
to hang a film on

we want it sugar-coated

the dance is no dance,
scripts and mutilation

the old way.

# TRICYCLE

About this unhappiness:
Run out and stay a minute,
Roll up in a blanket.

That's how they looked,
Tied to no actual drift.

Spoons were put up for sale.

We stood in our back alleys,
Chagrin brilliant on our faces.

I don't know.  Why does one write?

I replied to your waking
And the affair of sleeping and waking began.

Look, a fish is coming to save us.

Maybe unimportance isn't such a bad thing after all.

# MUTT AND JEFF

Actually the intent of
The polish remained,
A fragment of someone's snowball.

And you see, things work for me,
kind of. We get exported
and must scrabble around for a while
in some dusty square.

Wabash . . .

Still, the goldfish bowl remains
After all these years like an image
Reflected on water.

The mouse eyes me admiringly
From behind his chair; the one or two cats
Pass gravely under my leg from time to time.

My sudden fruiting into the war
Is like a dream now. The day

Bounced green off its boards.
There's nothing to return, really:

I saw my chance for a siesta and took it.

# IN ANOTHER TIME

Actually it was because you stopped
as though to embarrass the idea of stopping.

Light swelled, slivers, then listened.

Powdered suburban description
isn't precisely it. No briskness, cartoon
era of my early life.

What's printed on this thing?

Cars were discharging patrons
in front of theaters. It is no doubt
a slicker portrait
than you could have wished, yet all
the major aspects are present.

Bend down, waterfall
in the moss. It all came to life,

but quietly, there to transcribe it.

## EROTIC DOUBLE

He says he doesn't feel well
Here in the shade, one kind of old feeling.

The wordplay gets very intense,
Feelings to things.

Another go round?

Rescue me before the night does.

Barge made of ice, fissures of starlight
Keep us awake, dreams
As they happen.

I can hide it.  I choose to.
You.  You are a very pleasant person.

# Not worth dying for

I placed an ad
of the sight of women sewing in darkness

at table one
there are acres of us looking lewd
but respectful
like money in the bank

screw the mirrors
in each of us

dogs came after the dead called

the new intensity is landscaped
for lovemaking and lies

# Otherwise

Who would believe we cry
little girls pretending
to understand

they talk like adults

my poem was a lacquered thing
inflicted on those
trying to drum up business

recklessly one's family
made one forcing oneself
exactly what is required here

let's pass the others
knowing just out of the
way a finger told your story better

# Your original want list

Although children are counterfeit
there can be safety in numbers:

each of us wants and that matters,
we can stand anger

our speech not us or worse,
the pro romantic rope of our years together.

The moon is old, the closing of magic—
No one can find it pretty,

Terror and the lake,
All that glint in someone's eye,

It's what you are.  So stay
In the afternoon habit, crowd

At rest, star-gin in the mist
Who say it was nothing fun, a memory trap.

3

# THE WHITE SHIRT

(an Ashbery poem, erased, rearranged)

But if it wasn't for changes
Where would we go? Just
Having the illusion is enough.
But charge for it;
Serve immediately.

Thing of the past,
You in your growing,
Limits,
My working place.
The band is up.

The dry shore. A combustion engine
Means it's not working.

Suddenly all is quiet again.
I want to talk about something.
Attention? It's not that easy.

# A SEDENTARY EXISTENCE

Sometimes the truth—that thing

What could it have been
To be more or less

like writing a book disgusting.

Because we can do it. There's a freshness
to the air.

To be more or less unraveling
kindness
the look, the ticket. It is the expression

you know we keep an eye on

today. a speeding ship

# LOCAL TIME

What except
The hand is ours?

Gray eclipse, ill, the lilies
Arrive and the models

Undress, misread, confess.

Eat the toy.

Skulking aroma, neither of us gets
To know it's winter.

White is our harvest,
Good in the roar of old things.

# JUST WHAT'S THERE

He arrived sleepy
belabored by

chance

a pose I believe in

beer in the dormer
old guts of contraband:

a horse worships anything

a bag of nuts
long sounds in the corner of strange cities

The tedious process of ending ticks

there are sky
booths in the

breath somewhere

# And though people keep cutting in

they do resign

No point in taking the moment away

in the grass, chirping,
the bench so inviting

a leap into the middle of a dream

striking natural wonders

but, OK

in town there's a grist mill

that part of the dream

like a ship undone,
sails a blast of trombone

Now the daggers swamp green sky

and you complain

the women sob
and appoint you
diagonal

it is the custom here

pull down most of my face

The hats in the manuscript
were so fraternal

# On a nameless road

I flash merrily
when people think

if only we could get the cows

to consider voting

like the sky
or our faces

lean, empty mind

washed and arbitrary
shades that promise

a water table.

I don't know if I'll ever look young

pitiful morning,
sooner or later,
one's apertures

start looking disingenuous

desire is never enough

# Of pebbles obscured

our lard, in some cases
replicating

miniature to a fault

satisfy reports

we imagine as inexplicable

birth as a lot of hammering

   Then a blonde woman
   mistakenly assumed
   the thunder for a repertory of cries

damn of the earth

in whose rank

Feathers,

then personality,

were to be
argued

to a dead-end in the quietism
of the infinite

last peace . . .

## Inside other

roll of the snow

shoots up

a warrant is exchanged
in a great hiss of fire ants

the pathetic life force

is last to go home

but my kid is different

nobody would mess with her clams

therefore we can attack

we were interested
in having already done it
behind them

One scholar observes two people

her name was covered up

# A HELD THING

He sorted
what I know
you mean

so men become clarity
suck us out of the teenager

I cried
on a canvas

a vivid approximation of communion
reason and madness

that orchard
will make you think of time

for starters

but the rounded human
like a statistic in the good old days
makes the hood

of that bonnet
fall like a city

o little explosions when you need protection--

It's beginning

# SPOTLIGHT ON AMERICA

I must prod unflustered.
I hop around.

After all, hopping
I think
is like a big stranger in the mind.

Dr. Venetian blinds these animals.

Today pie fat in the whirlpool
of a few old pros.

Let the passing men be
the last to know us.

# DINOSAUR COUNTRY

Satin words, the strangest sins decline

Everyone happens tomorrow!

Now I'm an island self selected

I thought no one knew
about the pact between me and women:

"My dwelling place is your oven"

And then there was your wrist on my whispered Roman:

they'd done that
dinosaur
a moment of pleasure

you flash your shit
in the country
hold on

there are shadows
but you pay

you get even

# THE DECLINE OF THE WEST

the child ignores the horse
afraid to refute it

in the unconscious a weasel
grants you
stark theories

a person eats the bodies

and the hour wanders

dead ridinghood caught in a book

I saw His theory though,
my song

and now We are changed

# WET CASEMENTS

The conception: see as he streams
the look of diet impressions

self overlaid by

Ghost cosmetics

The shoes point (drifting)
Like a surface pierced

opinions as snapshots

you crow and some persons
named in his wallet crumble

I want very much that anger

a bridge like a dance for the bridge I face
not in water but in the stone bridge I keep for myself

not others

# Heaven

I almost meant people could
change an idea
                together

package it

the genius anyway
understands

I'm not going drunk

back to the dollhouse

young at lunch, harmless

gentleman

in the hall
*go back to the kitchen*

I knew the morning had passed

I could bow like a plastered
ad to the future

dripping

innate

# STUNG BY SOMETHING

my vice is comfort

a naïve story

and the current tragedy of priorities

the end of your pleasure
with girls—

they have so many bones—

couldn't happen

her front door knew my name

tree-house laughter
and mist

ten visits to reason
and an eternity of silence

her floors are not enough

embroidered departure we have heard about strangers

the pleasure

# Quite a few

a road spiked
with blue destinations

where a stranger deepens

silent now

so what to make of it
belonging under this plain wooden association

don't try to pass if off
as a canker

burn in the memory, a lever
for a new age of being

the day must start in poetry,
graves of sand,
the dead entirely attached, a small, other way of living


the wind?

the sound any creature has to spirit for a moment

and hope?

we perceive the animal

4

# LIVELONG DAYS

I sat at my desk, blasted

There was living in her young sister,
that precedence

and time
scrolled-up

everything living
in an answer

the whispering was cold

the occasion noticed a ghost
draft under the door

the painted stars were invisible
in the summer weeds

provisions constructed as a way of being

I won't tip
the book just as
the door is closing

I eat angels

something slight, different

inexact as longing
or myth

# Fit under here

I remember a ship

Dammit, I meant all along
I should take that other child

presently care is a hat

a father looking out the window

time's just a driveway,
the parrot said, staring into
the thudding fog

and the future is a salesman
with his name tag flying in a void

# Festival Asia

I first heard groans

shuttered distances and love

to repeat

we all wanted that

*bring the being*

I say go for some grants

be a trestle idle against the empty bellies

jobs we still maintain

you are a deadly white prisoner

pleasant once the future has had its way with hell

that's the way it is

a tangled diagram you can't excuse

caught, they all said

but that was the gin

a nice place to be

and more hogs were brought down

the owner of the rain was angry

# BALTIMORE

We live around
the saddest snow

Prairie metamorphosis

is this your company,
a curled up clock

of words

Collected     tho     licked

henbane presuming, I know

he spotted the child

everything

everything

I'm too shy to row away

# COP AND SWEATER

It's this thing
we beginners get in on

Once the face
no longer forgets

No homes on our backs

Sometimes in
long pauses

the elementary in mind
house so many of the others

the sick
stay away

a darkling few
wait with the buttons

a man could smash

into a
bird
person

an oasis of waiting to know

back here other moons
release happiness

the wine is a rain barrel!

Peace to the living we are to be more than

# THE WHOLE IS ADMIRABLY COMPOSED

a face looks up shore
blank and unconcerned

the lonely face sobs grieving

I bet you know
how he forgot

ill with water amid smooth boulders

now this envy

the challenge a dunce
shares around the real boy

you want the inconstant smile

a human tree again
that leads you to forget him

## MY GOLD CHAIN

Un Green the Diva
diamond . . .

her past

and the men's room thereof

I can't help being a little peon

she hollered at me
to forget
being meat on the butchers' scales

But then a dory enters the bridesmaid

The things you think you love

the question is so dark sometimes

# FALLS TO THE FLOOR, COMES TO THE DOOR

Arrival, taste as a statistic

The opera that wasn't there when I last looked

Matter like a tiny window or a bit of hope

The spring dream of
An elf on my back, the trunk
Becoming the world

Galaxies out in the street

It was I you answered
I see land not space

Luck sad under the bell

The past aches

# THE SPACIOUS FIRMAMENT

the people walk, burning

back to whoever took one reddish
unfazed note
for all the foxglove angels

give us what we bargained for

chumps and ferrets

a piss hall during the week

kilts out toiling, no force

going out in the nursery till time
is a grown man

it's true, a great fullness
waited at the end of my cobbled context


Capitalist runoff

villages blossom on wasps


just come

be my dance professor

# A DRIFTWOOD ALTAR

I like you, no question
your body a down payment;

the future is a drifter

consensus, polite indifference in young adults

remember?

I caught him shitting on meaning

the emptiness a sadness,
a pagan alert

a bathroom considerable with sludge

a chilly late remembering

they wore their coats
in certain precincts

washed and small

and people spilled their standard attitudes, no escape

certainly you must have
known all this,

the birds banging a promise
just as they did before the airplanes

the wind cracking,
indecent in the mirror

god of the trees
stop time

There has to be
animals expectant
in the doorways and windows

# THE LAST ROMANTIC

tell me about the waves

the world we made

you must be a gigolo
lost over the fact
you knew he was coming

once I said nobody believes you,
too many complicated leaks,
people who are normal

glue that includes children

My being did your quiet "European"
the way you always insisted

one other person is not a great distance

one block
in one ward
of the city

# THE EARTH-TONE MADONNA

What were you
telling about veins

implanted in everyone

forever

like meat
one could run around on?

There were peepers in the chaos
and not much else.

And if it's Wednesday?

The egrets snowplow
our workshoes.

David Dodd Lee is the author of six books of poems, including *The Nervous Filaments* (Four Way Books, 2010), *Orphan, Indiana* (University of Akron Press, 2010), and *Abrupt Rural* (New Issues, 2004).